contents

POWER OF THE
Pantry

Getting a meal on the table every night is so much easier when you have the right ingredients on hand. If you keep these ingredients in your cupboard, refrigerator or freezer, you'll always be able to cook the delicious recipes in this cookbook for your family at a moment's notice.

Breads

- ✓ Bread crumbs (plain and Italian-seasoned)
- ✓ Pepperidge Farm® breads
- ✓ Pepperidge Farm® Herb-Seasoned Stuffing

Dairy Foods

- ✓ Butter
- ✓ Eggs
- ✓ Milk
- ✓ Cheese (Swiss, fresh mozzarella, Parmesan or American)
- ✓ Shredded cheese (Cheddar, mozzarella, Monterey Jack or two-cheese blend)
- ✓ Heavy cream
- ✓ Sour cream

Fresh Produce

- ✓ Fresh fruit (bananas, kiwis, lemons, pears or red grapes)
- ✓ Fresh berries (strawberries, raspberries or blueberries)
- ✓ Fresh vegetables (asparagus, broccoli or red or green peppers)
- ✓ Fresh vegetables (carrots or celery)
- ✓ Fresh vegetables (cucumbers, snow peas or spinach)
- ✓ Garlic
- ✓ Onions (red, white, green)
- ✓ Potatoes
- ✓ Tomatoes

Freezer Foods

- ✓ Pepperidge Farm® Puff Pastry (shells and sheets)
- ✓ Vanilla ice cream

- ✓ Vegetables (peas, carrots, corn, mixed vegetables or chopped broccoli)
- ✓ Vegetables (cut green beans or spinach leaves)
- ✓ Whipped topping

Grocery Items

Baking

- ✓ Flour/cornstarch
- ✓ Nuts (pecans, macadamia or walnuts)
- ✓ Semi-sweet chocolate pieces
- ✓ Sugar (granulated, brown, confectioners')
- ✓ Vanilla extract

Grocery Items

Other

- ✓ Campbell's® condensed soups/broth
- ✓ Canned beans (white, black)
- ✓ Canned whole-kernel corn
- ✓ Canned diced tomatoes (regular and Italian-style)
- ✓ Canned fruit (pineapple chunks in juice, peach halves)
- ✓ Dijon-style mustard
- ✓ Egg noodles
- ✓ Flour tortillas
- ✓ Fruit juice/drinks (V8® V.Fusion™, V8 Splash®, orange juice)
- ✓ Honey
- ✓ Instant coffee
- ✓ Instant pudding mixes
- ✓ Mayonnaise
- ✓ Oils (olive, vegetable)
- ✓ Pace® Chunky Salsa
- ✓ Pace® Picante Sauce
- ✓ Pasta
- ✓ Prego® Italian Sauces
- ✓ Rice (regular, long-grain)
- ✓ Roasted sweet peppers

- ✓ Swanson® broths
- ✓ Tomato paste
- ✓ Vegetable cooking spray
- ✓ Vinegar (white wine)
- ✓ Wine (dry red, white)

Herbs and Spices

- ✓ Basil (dried and fresh)
- ✓ Bay leaf
- ✓ Black pepper (ground)
- ✓ Chili powder
- ✓ Cinnamon
- ✓ Crushed red pepper
- ✓ Cumin
- ✓ Dry mustard
- ✓ Garlic powder
- ✓ Ginger (ground)
- ✓ Italian seasoning
- ✓ Onion powder
- ✓ Oregano (dried or fresh)
- ✓ Paprika
- ✓ Parsley (dried or fresh)
- ✓ Rosemary (dried or fresh)
- ✓ Sage (fresh)
- ✓ Thyme (dried or fresh)

Meats, Poultry and Seafood

- ✓ Beef (beef for stew, short ribs)
- ✓ Beef (ground, sirloin)
- ✓ Fish (halibut, haddock or cod, tilapia or flounder)
- ✓ Poultry (skinless, boneless chicken breasts; turkey cutlets; ground turkey)
- ✓ Poultry (chicken parts, whole broiler-fryer, bone-in chicken breast halves)
- ✓ Pork (loin, chops)
- ✓ Shrimp
- ✓ Swanson® canned chicken
- ✓ Canned tuna

A well-stocked pantry can help you get these meals cooking in 10 minutes or less

Basil Shrimp Scampi

MAKES 6 SERVINGS

PREP
10 minutes

COOK
15 minutes

¼ cup olive oil

1½ pounds fresh large shrimp, shelled and deveined

1 tablespoon minced garlic

¼ teaspoon crushed red pepper

1½ cups Swanson® Chicken Broth (Regular, Natural Goodness™ **or** Certified Organic)

2 tablespoons lemon juice

½ cup thinly sliced fresh basil leaves

1 package (16 ounces) linguine, cooked and drained

¼ cup grated Parmesan cheese

1. Heat the oil in a 12-inch skillet over medium-high heat. Add the shrimp, garlic and red pepper and cook for 3 minutes or until the shrimp turn pink.

2. Stir the broth and juice into the skillet. Heat to a boil. Reduce the heat to low. Cook for 2 minutes. Stir in the basil, linguine and cheese. Cook and stir until the mixture is hot and bubbling. Serve with additional cheese, if desired.

Baked Crispy Chicken

PREP
10 minutes

BAKE
20 minutes

1 can (10¾ ounces) Campbell's® Condensed Cream of Chicken Soup (Regular **or** 98% Fat Free)

½ cup milk

4 skinless, boneless chicken breast halves

2 tablespoons all-purpose flour

1½ cups Pepperidge Farm® Herb Seasoned Stuffing, finely crushed

2 tablespoons butter, melted

1. Stir ⅓ **cup** of the soup and ¼ **cup** of the milk in a shallow dish. Lightly coat the chicken with the flour. Dip the chicken into the soup mixture, then coat with the stuffing.

2. Put the chicken on a baking sheet. Drizzle with the butter. Bake at 400°F. for 20 minutes or until the chicken is cooked through.

3. Heat the remaining soup and milk in a 1-quart saucepan over medium heat until hot, stirring occasionally. Serve the sauce with the chicken.

Bistro-Style Short Ribs

PREP
10 minutes

COOK
15 minutes

BAKE
1 hour
30 minutes

Vegetable cooking spray

3 pounds beef short ribs, cut into individual rib pieces

1 large onion, chopped (about 1 cup)

2 medium carrots, chopped (about ⅔ cup)

1 stalk celery, chopped (about ½ cup)

1 jar (1 pound 10 ounces) Prego® Traditional Italian Sauce

1¾ cups Swanson® Beef Broth (Regular, Lower Sodium **or** Certified Organic)

1. Spray an oven-safe 6-quart saucepot with cooking spray. Heat over medium-high heat for 1 minute. Cook the ribs in 2 batches or until they're browned on all sides. Remove the ribs with a slotted spoon and set aside. Pour off all but 2 tablespoons fat.

2. Add the onion, carrots and celery and cook until tender. Stir the sauce and broth into the saucepot. Heat to a boil. Return the ribs to the pot. Cover and bake at 350°F. for 1 hour 30 minutes or until the meat is fork-tender. Remove ribs with a fork or kitchen tongs from the cooker. Spoon off any fat from the sauce.

Slow Cooker Method: Brown the ribs in a 12-inch skillet as directed in step 1. Place the onion, carrots and celery in a 3½- to 6-quart slow cooker. Top with the ribs. Stir the sauce and broth into the cooker. Cover and cook on LOW for 7 to 8 hours* or until the meat is fork-tender. Remove ribs with a fork or kitchen tongs from the cooker. Spoon off any fat from the sauce.

*Or on HIGH for 3½ to 4 hours

Cheese-Stuffed Meatloaf

PREP
10 minutes

BAKE
1 hour

STAND
5 minutes

1½   pounds ground beef
1   jar (16 ounces) Pace® Chunky Salsa
⅓   cup plain dry bread crumbs
1   egg, beaten
1   cup shredded mozzarella cheese

1. Thoroughly mix the beef, ½ cup of the salsa, bread crumbs and egg in a large bowl. Put the mixture on a work surface and firmly shape beef mixture into a 12×8-inch rectangle.

2. Sprinkle the cheese down the center of the meat mixture, leaving ½-inch border on all sides. Roll up, starting at the long end, like a jelly roll. Press the ends together to seal. Place the meatloaf seam-side down in a 13×9×2-inch baking pan.

3. Bake at 350°F. for 45 minutes.

4. Pour the remaining salsa over the meatloaf. Bake for 15 minutes more or until the meatloaf is cooked through. Remove the meatloaf from the pan to a cutting board and let stand for 5 minutes before slicing.

12 QUICK-PREP MAIN DISHES

Shortcut Barbecued Chicken

PREP
5 minutes

GRILL
40 minutes

1   can (10¾ ounces) Campbell's® Condensed Tomato Soup

2   tablespoons honey

1   teaspoon dry mustard

½   teaspoon onion powder

4   bone-in chicken breast halves (about 2 pounds), skin removed

1. Stir the soup, honey, mustard and onion powder in a small bowl.

2. Lightly oil the grill rack and heat the grill to medium. Grill the chicken for 20 minutes, turning the chicken over halfway through cooking. Grill for 20 minutes more or until the chicken is cooked through, turning and brushing it with the soup mixture while grilling.

3. Heat the remaining soup mixture in a 1-quart saucepan over medium heat until it's hot and bubbling, stirring often. Serve with the chicken.

Broccoli-Cheese Chicken

PREP
5 minutes

COOK
20 minutes

1   tablespoon butter

4   skinless, boneless chicken breast halves

1   can (10¾ ounces) Campbell's® Condensed
     Broccoli Cheese Soup (Regular **or**
     98% Fat Free)

⅓   cup water

⅛   teaspoon ground black pepper

2   cups fresh **or** frozen broccoli flowerets

1. Heat the butter in a 10-inch skillet over medium-high heat. Add the chicken and cook for 10 minutes or until it's well browned on both sides. Remove the chicken and set aside.

2. Stir the soup, water, black pepper and broccoli into the skillet. Heat to a boil. Return the chicken to the skillet and reduce the heat to low. Cover and cook for 5 minutes or until the chicken is cooked through.

Grilled Beef Steak with Sautéed Onions

2   tablespoons olive oil

2   large onions, thinly sliced (about 2 cups)

2   pounds boneless beef sirloin, strip **or** rib
      steaks, cut into 8 pieces

1   jar (16 ounces) Pace® Chunky Salsa

PREP
5 minutes

COOK/GRILL
25 minutes

1. Heat **1 tablespoon** of the oil in a 12-inch skillet
over medium heat. Add the onions and cook until they're
tender. Remove the onions from the skillet and keep
warm.

2. Heat the remaining oil in the skillet. Add the steak
pieces and cook until they're well browned on both
sides.

3. Add the salsa and return the onions to the skillet.
Cook for 3 minutes for medium-rare or until desired
doneness.

Baked Fish with Lemon & Herbs

PREP

10 minutes

BAKE

20 minutes

2   slices Pepperidge Farm® Farmhouse™ Sourdough Bread, torn into pieces

2   tablespoons chopped fresh parsley

1   tablespoon grated lemon peel

½   cup mayonnaise

2   tablespoons lemon juice

6   fresh white fish fillets (tilapia **or** flounder)

    Vegetable cooking spray

1. Put the bread, parsley and lemon peel in an electric blender container. Cover and process until crumbs form.

2. Stir the mayonnaise with **1 tablespoon** of the lemon juice. Spread the mayonnaise mixture on the fillets. Sprinkle with the bread crumb mixture. Arrange the fillets on a baking sheet. Spray with cooking spray.

3. Bake at 425°F. for 20 minutes or until the fish flakes easily when tested with a fork. Sprinkle with remaining lemon juice before serving.

Lemon Broccoli Chicken

1 lemon

1 tablespoon vegetable oil

4 skinless, boneless chicken breast halves

1 can (10¾ ounces) Campbell's® Condensed Cream of Broccoli Soup (Regular **or** 98% Fat Free)

¼ cup milk

⅛ teaspoon ground black pepper

PREP
5 minutes

COOK
20 minutes

1. Cut **4** thin slices of lemon. Squeeze 2 teaspoons juice from the remaining lemon.

2. Heat the oil in a 10-inch skillet over medium-high heat. Add the chicken and cook for 10 minutes or until it's well browned on both sides. Remove the chicken and set aside.

3. Stir the soup, milk, lemon juice and black pepper into the skillet. Heat to a boil. Return the chicken to the skillet and reduce the heat to low. Top the chicken with the lemon slices. Cover and cook for 5 minutes or until the chicken is cooked through.

Savory Pork and Vegetables

PREP

10 minutes

COOK

30 minutes

2 tablespoons butter

4 boneless pork chops, ¾-inch thick

1½ cups sliced mushrooms (about 4 ounces)

½ teaspoon dried rosemary leaves, crushed

1 can (10¾ ounces) Campbell's® Condensed Cream of Mushroom Soup (Regular **or** 98% Fat Free)

2 tablespoons water

1 package (9 ounces) frozen cut green beans

4 cups medium egg noodles, cooked and drained

1. Heat **1 tablespoon** of the butter in a 10-inch skillet over medium-high heat. Add the pork chops and cook until well browned on both sides. Remove the chops and set aside.

2. Reduce the heat to medium and add the remaining butter. Add the mushrooms and rosemary. Cook and stir until tender and the liquid is evaporated.

3. Stir the soup, water and beans into the skillet. Heat to a boil. Return the chops to the skillet. Reduce the heat to low. Cover and cook for 10 minutes or until the chops are cooked through and beans are tender, stirring occasionally. Serve with the noodles.

Poached Fish with Pineapple Salsa

PREP
10 minutes

COOK
15 minutes

1   can (15¼ ounces) pineapple chunks in juice, undrained

1   seedless cucumber, peeled and diced (about 1⅔ cups)

1   medium red pepper, chopped (about ¾ cup)

2   tablespoons chopped red onion

1   teaspoon white wine vinegar

⅛   teaspoon crushed red pepper (optional)

1¾ cups Swanson® Chicken Broth (Regular, Natural Goodness™ **or** Certified Organic)

¼   cup white wine

4   fresh white fish fillets (halibut, haddock **or** cod)

1. Drain the pineapple and reserve ⅔ **cup** of the juice.

2. Mix the pineapple chunks, cucumber, red pepper, red onion, vinegar and crushed red pepper, if desired in a medium bowl and set aside.

3. Heat the broth, wine and reserved pineapple juice in a 12-inch skillet over high heat to a boil. Add the fish and reduce the heat to low. Cover and cook for 10 minutes or until the fish flakes easily when tested with a fork. Serve the fish with the pineapple salsa.

Skillet Pork Chops Florentine

PREP
5 minutes

COOK
30 minutes

2 tablespoons olive **or** vegetable oil

6 boneless pork chops, ¾-inch thick

1 medium onion, sliced thin (about ½ cup)

1 jar (1 pound 9 ounces) Prego® Marinara Italian Sauce

1 package (10 ounces) frozen leaf spinach, thawed and well drained

1 cup shredded mozzarella cheese (4 ounces)

TIME-SAVING TIP

To thaw spinach, microwave on HIGH 3 minutes, breaking apart with a fork halfway through heating.

---

1. Heat **1 tablespoon** of the oil in a 12-inch skillet over medium-high heat. Add the pork chops and cook until the chops are well browned on both sides. Remove the pork chops and set aside.

2. Reduce the heat to medium and add the remaining oil. Add the onion. Cook and stir until the onion is tender-crisp.

3. Stir the Italian sauce and spinach into the skillet. Heat to a boil. Return the pork chops to the skillet and reduce the heat to low. Cover and cook until the chops are cooked through. Sprinkle with the cheese.

Saucy Pork Chops

MAKES 4 SERVINGS

1 tablespoon vegetable oil

4 bone-in pork chops, ½-inch thick

1 can (10¾ ounces) Campbell's® Condensed Cream of Onion Soup

¼ cup water

PREP
5 minutes

COOK
20 minutes

1. Heat the oil in a 10-inch skillet over medium-high heat. Add the pork chops and cook until the chops are well browned on both sides.

2. Stir the soup and water into the skillet. Heat to a boil. Reduce the heat to low. Cover and cook for 10 minutes or until the chops are cooked through but slightly pink in center.

Best Ever Meatloaf

PREP

10 minutes

BAKE

1 hour 15 to
30 minutes

STAND

10 minutes

2   pounds ground beef

1   can (10¾ ounces) Campbell's® Condensed
       Cream of Mushroom Soup (Regular
       or 98% Fat Free)

½   cup fine dry bread crumbs

1   egg, beaten

1   small onion, finely chopped (about ¼ cup)

⅓   cup water

1. Thoroughly mix the beef, ½ **cup** of the soup, bread
crumbs, egg and onion in a large bowl. Put the mixture
into a 13×9×2-inch baking pan and firmly shape into
a 8×4-inch loaf.

2. Bake at 350°F. for 1 hour 15 minutes to 1 hour
30 minutes or until the meatloaf is cooked through.
Remove the meatloaf with a slotted spatula to a cutting
board. Let the meatloaf stand for 10 minutes before
slicing.

3. Heat **1 tablespoon** of the pan drippings and the
remaining soup and water in a 1-quart saucepan over
medium-high heat to a boil. Serve with the meatloaf.

All in One Dish

Casseroles and one dish meals are a natural when you're cooking out of the pantry

Rosemary Chicken & Roasted Vegetables

PREP
15 minutes

BAKE
1 hour
30 minutes

3-pound whole broiler-fryer chicken
1   tablespoon butter, melted
4   medium red potatoes, cut into quarters
2   cups fresh **or** frozen baby carrots
2   stalks celery, cut into chunks
12   small white onions, peeled
½   teaspoon dried rosemary leaves, crushed
1   cup Swanson® Chicken Broth (Regular, Natural Goodness™ **or** Certified Organic)
½   cup orange juice

TIME·SAVING TIP

To quickly peel onions, pour boiling water over onions and let stand for 5 minutes. Then slip off skins.

1. Brush the chicken with the butter. Place the chicken, potatoes, carrots, celery and onions in a roasting pan. Sprinkle with rosemary. Stir the broth and orange juice in a small bowl and pour **half** of the broth mixture over the chicken and vegetables.

2. Bake at 375°F. for 1 hour.

3. Stir the vegetables. Add the remaining broth mixture to the pan. Bake for 30 minutes more or until the chicken is cooked through.

Beef and Mozzarella Bake

PREP
10 minutes

COOK
35 minutes

1 pound ground beef

1 teaspoon dried basil leaves, crushed

¼ teaspoon ground black pepper

⅛ teaspoon garlic powder **or** 1 clove garlic, minced

1¼ cups Prego® Traditional Italian Sauce

1 can (10¾ ounces) Campbell's® Condensed Cream of Mushroom Soup (Regular **or** 98% Fat Free)

1¼ cups water

1½ cups shredded mozzarella cheese (6 ounces)

3 cups medium shell-shaped pasta, cooked and drained

1. Cook the beef, basil, black pepper and garlic powder in a 10-inch skillet over medium-high heat until well browned, stirring frequently to break up meat. Pour off any fat.

2. Stir the sauce, soup, water and **1 cup** of the mozzarella cheese into the skillet. Stir in the pasta to coat with the sauce mixture. Spoon into a 11×8-inch (2-quart) shallow baking dish. Sprinkle with the remaining cheese.

3. Bake at 400°F. for 25 minutes or until hot and bubbling.

Beef & Mushroom Dijon

PREP
10 minutes

COOK
25 minutes

Vegetable cooking spray

2 cups sliced mushrooms

1 medium onion, chopped (about ½ cup)

¾ pound boneless beef sirloin, ¾-inch thick, cut into thin strips

1 can (10¾ ounces) Campbell's® Healthy Request® Condensed Cream of Mushroom Soup

¼ cup water

2 tablespoons Dijon-style mustard

4 cups hot cooked rice, cooked without salt

Chopped fresh parsley

1. Spray a 10-inch skillet with cooking spray and heat over medium-high heat for 1 minute. Add the mushrooms and onion and cook until tender. Remove the vegetables. Remove skillet from the heat.

2. Spray the skillet with cooking spray. Add the beef and cook until well browned and juices evaporate, stirring often.

3. Stir the soup, water, mustard and vegetables into the skillet. Cook and stir until hot and bubbly. Toss rice with parsley.

Chicken-Mushroom Risotto

PREP

10 minutes

COOK

35 minutes

Vegetable cooking spray

¾ pound skinless, boneless chicken breasts, cut into cubes

1 small onion, finely chopped (about ¼ cup)

1 small carrot, chopped (about ¼ cup)

1 cup **uncooked** regular long-grain white rice

1¾ cups Swanson® Chicken Broth (Regular, Natural Goodness™ **or** Certified Organic)

1 can (10¾ ounces) Campbell's® Healthy Request® Condensed Cream of Mushroom Soup

⅛ teaspoon ground black pepper

½ cup frozen peas

1. Spray a 10-inch skillet with cooking spray and heat over medium-high heat for 1 minute. Add the chicken and cook until it's well browned, stirring often. Remove the chicken and set aside.

2. Reduce the heat to medium. Add the onion, carrot and rice. Cook and stir until the rice is browned.

3. Stir the broth, soup and black pepper into the skillet. Heat to a boil. Reduce the heat to low. Cover and cook for 15 minutes.

4. Stir in the peas and return the chicken to the skillet. Cover and cook for 5 minutes more or until the chicken is cooked through and the rice is tender.

Creamy Chicken Enchiladas

PREP
   20 minutes

BAKE
   40 minutes

1   can (10¾ ounces) Campbell's® Condensed
      Cream of Chicken Soup (Regular
      or 98% Fat Free)

1   container (8 ounces) sour cream

1   cup Pace® Picante Sauce

2   teaspoons chili powder

2   cups chopped cooked chicken

1   cup shredded Monterey Jack cheese
      (4 ounces)

10 flour tortillas (8-inch), warmed

1   medium tomato, chopped

1   medium green onion, sliced (about
      2 tablespoons)

1. Stir the soup, sour cream, picante sauce and chili powder in a small bowl.

2. Stir **1 cup** of the soup mixture, chicken and cheese in a medium bowl.

3. Spread **about ¼ cup** of the chicken mixture down the center of each tortilla. Roll up and place seam-side down in a 13×9×2-inch shallow baking dish. Pour remaining soup mixture over the enchiladas. **Cover**.

4. Bake at 350°F. for 40 minutes or until hot. Top with tomato and green onion.

Crunchy Chicken Bake

PREP
10 minutes

BAKE
25 minutes

8   skinless, boneless chicken breast halves

4   slices Swiss cheese (about 4 ounces),
    cut in half

1   can (10¾ ounces) Campbell's® Condensed
    Cream of Broccoli Soup (Regular **or**
    98% Fat Free)

1   large tomato, cut into 8 slices

½   cup Pepperidge Farm® Herb Seasoned
    Stuffing, crushed

2   tablespoons butter, melted

    Hot cooked rice

1. Place the chicken in a 13×9×2-inch shallow baking dish. Top each chicken breast with **1** piece cheese. Spoon the soup over the cheese. Arrange the tomato over the soup.

2. Mix the stuffing with the butter in a small cup and sprinkle over the tomato.

3. Bake at 400°F. for 25 minutes or until the chicken is cooked through. Serve with rice.

Chicken Noodle Casserole

PREP
10 minutes

BAKE
25 minutes

1 can (10¾ ounces) Campbell's® Condensed Cream of Chicken Soup (Regular **or** 98% Fat Free)

½ cup milk

1 cup frozen peas

2 cans (4.5 ounces **each**) Swanson® Premium Chunk Chicken Breast, drained

2 cups medium egg noodles, cooked and drained

2 tablespoons dry bread crumbs

1 tablespoon butter, melted

1. Stir the soup, milk, peas, chicken and noodles in a 1½-quart casserole.

2. Bake at 400°F. for 20 minutes or until hot. Stir.

3. Mix the bread crumbs with the butter in a small cup and sprinkle over the chicken mixture. Bake for 5 minutes more or until the topping is golden brown.

Tuscan Turkey & Beans

PREP

10 minutes

COOK

20 minutes

2 tablespoons olive **or** vegetable oil

4 turkey breast cutlets

1 medium onion, chopped (about ½ cup)

2 cloves garlic, minced

1½ teaspoons dried Italian seasoning, crushed

1 can (about 14½ ounces) diced tomatoes, undrained

1½ cups packed chopped fresh spinach leaves

1 can (10¾ ounces) Campbell's® Condensed Cream of Celery Soup (Regular **or** 98% Fat Free)

¼ teaspoon ground black pepper

1 can (about 16 ounces) white kidney (cannellini) beans, rinsed and drained

Grated Parmesan cheese

1. Heat **1 tablespoon** of the oil in a 12-inch skillet over medium-high heat. Add the turkey in 2 batches and cook for 3 minutes or until lightly browned. Remove the turkey and set aside.

2. Reduce the heat to medium and add the remaining oil. Add the onion, garlic and Italian seasoning. Cook and stir until the onion is tender-crisp.

3. Add the tomatoes and spinach. Cook and stir just until the spinach wilts. Stir the soup, black pepper and beans into the skillet. Heat to a boil. Return the turkey to the skillet and reduce the heat to low. Cover and cook for 5 minutes or until the turkey is cooked through. Sprinkle with the cheese.

Margherita-Style Pizza

PREP
5 minutes

COOK
10 minutes

2 slices Pepperidge Farm® 9- or 15-Grain Natural Whole Grain Bread

Vegetable cooking spray

½ teaspoon dried oregano leaves, crushed

2 medium plum tomatoes, thinly sliced

2 ounces fresh mozzarella cheese, cut up

6 fresh basil leaves, thinly shredded

1. Spray top of each bread slice with cooking spray and sprinkle with oregano.

2. Heat a 10-inch skillet over medium heat for 1 minute. Put the bread slices, oregano-side down in the skillet. Cook until they're lightly browned. Turn bread slices over.

3. Divide the tomatoes and cheese between the bread slices. Cover and cook until the cheese softens. Sprinkle with basil.

Tuna Rice Casserole

1   can (10¾ ounces) Campbell's® Condensed Cream of Mushroom Soup (Regular **or** 98% Fat Free)

1½ cups milk

¼   teaspoon paprika

     Dash ground red pepper

2   cans (about 6 ounces **each**) tuna, drained

4   ounces sliced American cheese, cut up (about 1 cup)

¾   cup **uncooked** regular long-grain white rice

2   tablespoons dry bread crumbs

1   tablespoon butter, melted

PREP
10 minutes

BAKE
50 minutes

1. Stir the soup, milk, paprika, red pepper, tuna, cheese and rice in a 9-inch square baking dish. **Cover.**

2. Bake at 350°F. for 30 minutes. Stir.

3. Mix the bread crumbs with the butter in a small cup and sprinkle over the tuna mixture. Bake for 20 minutes more or until hot and bubbly and the rice is tender.

Shrimp & Rice Scampi

PREP
15 minutes

COOK
25 minutes

2 cups **uncooked** instant white rice

3½ cups Swanson® Chicken Broth (Regular, Natural Goodness™ **or** Certified Organic), heated

3 tablespoons lemon juice

4 cloves garlic, minced

2 medium green onions, thinly sliced (about ¼ cup)

1 pound fresh **or** frozen large shrimp, shelled and deveined

1. Put the rice in an 8-inch square baking dish. Stir in the broth, lemon juice, garlic and green onions. Top with the shrimp. **Cover**.

2. Bake at 400°F. for 25 minutes or until the rice is tender and the shrimp turn pink.

Monterey Chicken Fajitas

MAKES 8 FAJITAS

2	tablespoons vegetable oil
1	pound skinless, boneless chicken breasts, cut into strips
1	medium green pepper, cut into 2-inch-long strips (about 1½ cups)
1	medium onion, sliced (about ½ cup)
1	can (10¾ ounces) Campbell's® Condensed Cream of Mushroom Soup (Regular **or** 98% Fat Free)
½	cup Pace® Chunky Salsa
8	flour tortillas (8-inch), warmed
1	cup shredded Monterey Jack cheese (4 ounces)

PREP
15 minutes

COOK
15 minutes

1. Heat the oil in a 10-inch skillet over medium-high heat. Add the chicken and cook until it's well browned, stirring often.

2. Reduce the heat to medium. Add the pepper and onion. Cook and stir until the vegetables are tender-crisp. Stir the soup and salsa into the skillet. Cook until the chicken is cooked through.

3. Spoon about ½ **cup** of the chicken mixture down the center of each tortilla. Top with the cheese and additional salsa. Fold the tortilla around the filling.

Savory Chicken and Mushrooms

PREP
15 minutes

COOK
25 minutes

2 tablespoons butter

4 skinless, boneless chicken breast halves

1½ cups fresh broccoli flowerets

1½ cups sliced fresh mushrooms (about 4 ounces)

1 can (10¾ ounces) Campbell's® Condensed Cream of Chicken Mushroom Soup

¼ cup milk

2 tablespoons Dijon-style mustard

4 cups medium egg noodles, cooked and drained

Red grapes **and** fresh sage leaves for garnish (optional)

1. Heat **1 tablespoon** butter in a 10-inch skillet over medium-high heat, cook chicken 10 minutes or until browned on both sides. Remove chicken and set aside.

2. Reduce the heat to medium. Add the remaining butter. Add the broccoli and mushrooms and cook until the vegetables are tender and liquid is evaporated, stirring often.

3. Stir the soup, milk and mustard into the skillet. Heat to a boil. Return the chicken to the skillet and reduce the heat to low. Cover and cook for 5 minutes or until the chicken is cooked through. Serve with the noodles. Garnish with grapes and sage, if desired.

Pork with Roasted Peppers & Potatoes

MAKES 4 SERVINGS

4 boneless pork chops, ½-inch thick
Ground black pepper

1 tablespoon olive oil

4 medium red potatoes (about 1 pound), cut into 1-inch pieces

1 medium onion, sliced (about ½ cup)

1 teaspoon dried oregano leaves, crushed

1 cup Swanson® Chicken Broth (Regular, Natural Goodness™ **or** Certified Organic)

½ cup diced roasted sweet peppers

PREP
10 minutes

COOK
25 minutes

1. Season the pork chops with the black pepper.

2. Heat the oil in a 10-inch skillet over medium-high heat. Add the pork chops and cook for 10 minutes or until browned on both sides. Remove the chops and set aside.

3. Add the potatoes, onion and oregano. Cook and stir for 5 minutes or until browned.

4. Stir the broth and sweet peppers into the skillet. Heat to a boil. Return the pork chops to the skillet and reduce the heat to low. Cover and cook for 10 minutes or until the chops are cooked through.

Savory Soups & Stews

Soups and stews are quick and easy to put together when your pantry is stocked well

Tuscan Beef Stew

MAKES 8 SERVINGS

PREP
15 minutes

COOK
8 to 9 hours

1 can (10¾ ounces) Campbell's® Condensed Tomato Soup

1 can (10½ ounces) Campbell's® Condensed Beef Broth

½ cup Burgundy **or** other dry red wine **or** water

1 teaspoon dried Italian seasoning, crushed

½ teaspoon garlic powder

1 can (14½ ounces) diced Italian-style tomatoes

3 large carrots, cut into 1-inch pieces (about 2¼ cups)

2 pounds beef for stew, cut into 1-inch pieces

2 cans (about 16 ounces **each**) white kidney (cannellini) beans, rinsed and drained

1. Stir the soup, broth, wine, Italian seasoning, garlic powder, tomatoes, carrots and beef in a 3½-quart slow cooker.

2. Cover and cook on LOW for 8 to 9 hours* or until the meat and vegetables are fork-tender.

3. Stir in the beans. Turn the heat to HIGH. Cook for 10 minutes more.

Or on HIGH for 4 to 5 hours

Black Bean, Corn & Turkey Chili

PREP

5 minutes

COOK

45 minutes

1   tablespoon vegetable oil

1   pound ground turkey

1   large onion, chopped (about 1 cup)

2   tablespoons chili powder

1   teaspoon ground cumin

1   teaspoon dried oregano leaves, crushed

½   teaspoon ground black pepper

¼   teaspoon garlic powder **or** 2 cloves garlic, minced

1¾   cups Swanson® Chicken Broth (Regular, Natural Goodness™ **or** Certified Organic)

1   cup Pace® Chunky Salsa

1   tablespoon sugar

1   can (about 15 ounces) black beans, rinsed and drained

1   package (16 ounces) frozen whole kernel corn

1. Heat the oil in a 4-quart saucepan over medium-high heat. Add the turkey, onion, chili powder, cumin, oregano, black pepper and garlic powder. Cook until turkey is well browned, stirring frequently to break up meat.

2. Stir the broth, salsa, sugar, beans and corn into the saucepan. Heat to a boil. Reduce the heat to low.

3. Cover and cook for 30 minutes. Stir the chili occasionally while cooking.

Spaghetti Soup

PREP
15 minutes

COOK
30 minutes

2 tablespoons vegetable oil

½ pound skinless, boneless chicken breasts, cut into cubes

1 medium onion, chopped (about ½ cup)

1 large carrot, chopped (about ½ cup)

1 stalk celery, finely chopped (about ⅓ cup)

2 cloves garlic, minced

4 cups Swanson® Chicken Broth (Regular, Natural Goodness™ **or** Certified Organic)

1 can (10¾ ounces) Campbell's® Condensed Tomato Soup

1 cup water

3 ounces **uncooked** spaghetti, broken into 1-inch pieces

2 tablespoons chopped fresh parsley (optional)

1. Heat **1 tablespoon** of the oil in a 6-quart saucepot over medium-high heat. Add the chicken and cook until it's well browned, stirring often. Remove the chicken.

2. Reduce the heat to medium and add the remaining oil. Add the onion and cook for 1 minute. Add the carrots and cook for 1 minute. Add the celery and garlic and cook for 1 minute.

3. Stir the broth, soup and water into the saucepot. in the pasta. Cook for 10 minutes or until the pasta is tender. Add the chicken and parsley, if desired, and heat through.

Tomato Florentine Chicken Stew

PREP

10 minutes

COOK

55 minutes

1	tablespoon vegetable oil
2½	pounds chicken parts
1	large onion, sliced (about 1 cup)
4	garlic cloves, minced (2 tablespoons)
1	can (6 ounces) tomato paste
1	teaspoon dried basil leaves, crushed
1	teaspoon dried oregano leaves, crushed
½	teaspoon ground black pepper
3½	cups Swanson® Chicken Broth (Regular, Natural Goodness™ **or** Certified Organic)
1	bag (16 ounces) frozen spinach leaves **or** chopped spinach
¼	cup grated Parmesan cheese

1. Heat the oil in a 6-quart saucepot over medium-high heat. Cook the chicken in 2 batches or until well browned. Remove chicken and set aside.

2. Add the onion and cook over medium-low heat for 2 minutes. Stir the garlic, tomato paste, basil, oregano and black pepper into the saucepot. Cook for 2 minutes.

3. Add the broth. Heat to a boil. Return the chicken to the saucepot and reduce the heat to low. Cover and cook for 30 minutes.

4. Stir in the spinach and cheese. Cover and cook for 10 minutes more or until the chicken is cooked through.

Country Chicken with Lemon and Herbs

PREP
15 minutes

COOK
40 minutes

4	pounds chicken parts
½	cup all-purpose flour
1	tablespoon vegetable oil
2	stalks celery, coarsely chopped (about 1 cup)
1	large onion, cut into 8 wedges
½	pound baby carrots
1	lemon
1¾	cups Swanson® Chicken Broth (Regular, Natural Goodness™ **or** Certified Organic)
1	teaspoon dried rosemary leaves, crushed
	Hot cooked buttered egg noodles **or** mashed potatoes

1. Lightly coat the chicken with the flour. Heat the oil in a 6-quart saucepot over medium-high heat. Cook the chicken in 2 batches or until it's well browned. Remove the chicken and set aside.

2. Add the celery, onion and carrots to the saucepot and cook for 3 minutes.

3. Squeeze the juice from lemon (about ¼ cup). Stir the juice, broth and rosemary into the saucepot. Heat to a boil. Return the chicken to the pot and reduce the heat to low. Cover and cook for 40 minutes or until the chicken is cooked through and vegetables are tender. Serve with buttered noodles or mashed potatoes.

Hearty Beef Stew

PREP

10 minutes

COOK

2 hours

15 minutes

Vegetable cooking spray

1   pound beef for stew, cut into 1-inch pieces

1¾ cups Swanson® Beef Broth (Regular, Lower Sodium **or** Certified Organic)

1   bay leaf

½   teaspoon dried thyme leaves, crushed

⅛   teaspoon ground black pepper

3   medium carrots, cut into 1-inch pieces (about 1½ cups)

2   medium potatoes, cut into quarters

2   tablespoons all-purpose flour

¼   cup water

1. Spray a 6-quart saucepot with vegetable cooking spray and heat over medium-high heat for 1 minute. Add the beef and cook until it's well browned, stirring often. Pour off any fat.

2. Stir the broth, bay leaf, thyme and black pepper into the saucepot. Heat to a boil. Reduce the heat to low. Cover and cook for 1 hour 30 minutes.

3. Add the carrots and potatoes to the saucepot. Cover and cook for 30 minutes more or until the meat is fork-tender.

4. Stir the flour and water in a small bowl. Stir the flour mixture into the saucepot. Cook and stir until the mixture boils and thickens. Discard the bay leaf.

Slow Cooker Beef & Vegetable Soup

PREP
25 minutes

COOK
8 to 10 hours

1 pound beef for stew, cut into 1-inch pieces
Ground black pepper
2 tablespoons all-purpose flour
2 tablespoons vegetable oil
3 large onions, chopped (about 3 cups)
12 small red-skinned potatoes, cut into quarters
2 medium carrots, sliced (about 1 cup)
4 cloves garlic, minced
1 tablespoon chopped fresh thyme **or**
1 teaspoon dried thyme leaves, crushed
4 cups Swanson® Beef Broth (Regular, Lower Sodium **or** Certified Organic)
2 tablespoons tomato paste
1½ teaspoons instant coffee powder **or** granules
Sour cream (optional)
Chopped green onions (optional)

1. Season the beef with the black pepper and coat with flour. Heat the oil in a 10-inch skillet over medium-high heat. Add the beef and cook until it's well browned, stirring often.

2. Place the onions, potatoes, carrots, garlic and thyme in a 3½-quart slow cooker. Top with the beef. Stir **1 cup** of the broth, tomato paste and coffee in a small bowl. Pour the coffee mixture and remaining broth into the cooker.

3. Cover and cook on LOW for 8 to 10 hours* or until the meat is fork-tender. Serve with sour cream and green onions, if desired.

*Or on HIGH for 4 to 5 hours

Picante Pork Stew

3 tablespoons cornstarch

1¾ cups Swanson® Vegetable Broth (Regular **or** Certified Organic)

2 tablespoons vegetable oil

1 pound boneless pork loin, cut into thin strips

4 cups cut-up fresh vegetables*

½ cup Pace® Picante Sauce

PREP
20 minutes

COOK
25 minutes

1. Stir the cornstarch and broth in a small bowl. Set the mixture aside.

2. Heat **1 tablespoon** of the oil in a 6-quart saucepot over medium-high heat. Add the pork and cook until it's well browned, stirring often. Remove the pork with a slotted spoon and set aside.

3. Reduce the heat to medium. Add the remaining oil. Add the vegetables and cook until tender-crisp. Pour off any fat.

4. Add the picante sauce. Stir the cornstarch mixture and stir into the saucepot. Cook and stir until the mixture boils and thickens. Return the pork to the saucepot and heat through.

Use asparagus cut into 2-inch pieces, red pepper cut into 2-inch-long strips and sliced onions.

Southwestern Chicken & White Bean Soup

PREP

15 minutes

COOK

8 to 10 hours

1 tablespoon vegetable oil

1 pound skinless, boneless chicken breasts, cut into 1-inch pieces

1¾ cups Swanson® Chicken Broth (Regular, Natural Goodness™ **or** Certified Organic)

1 cup Pace® Chunky Salsa

3 cloves garlic, minced

2 teaspoons ground cumin

1 can (about 16 ounces) small white beans, rinsed and drained

1 cup frozen whole kernel corn

1 large onion, chopped (about 1 cup)

1. Heat the oil in a 10-inch skillet over medium-high heat. Add the chicken and cook until it's well browned, stirring often.

2. Stir the broth, salsa, garlic, cumin, beans, corn and onion in a 3½-quart slow cooker. Add the chicken.

3. Cover and cook on LOW for 8 to 10 hours* or until the chicken is cooked through.

Or on HIGH for 4 to 5 hours

Chicken & Pasta Stew

PREP

10 minutes

COOK

35 minutes

1 tablespoon cornstarch

1 tablespoon water

2 tablespoons vegetable oil

¾ pound skinless, boneless chicken breasts, cut into cubes

1 cup frozen sliced carrots

1 cup frozen cut green beans

¾ cup chopped onion

6 cups Swanson® Chicken Broth (Regular, Natural Goodness™ **or** Certified Organic)

1 cup **uncooked** bow tie-shaped pasta (farfalle)

2 tablespoons chopped fresh parsley (optional)

1. Stir the cornstarch and water in a small bowl. Set the mixture aside.

2. Heat **1 tablespoon** of the oil in a 4-quart saucepan over medium-high heat. Add the chicken and cook until it's well browned, stirring often. Remove the chicken with a slotted spoon and set aside.

3. Reduce the heat to medium. Add the remaining oil. Add the carrots, beans and onion and cook until tender-crisp.

4. Stir the broth into the saucepan. Heat to a boil. Add the pasta and parsley, if desired. Cook for 10 minutes or until the pasta is tender. Return the chicken to the saucepan and heat through.

5. Stir the cornstarch mixture and stir into the saucepan. Cook and stir until the mixture boils and thickens slightly.

Cheesy Chicken Chowder

1   can (10¾ ounces) Campbell's® Condensed
    Cheddar Cheese Soup

1   soup can milk

¾   cup Pace® Picante Sauce

1   small red **or** green pepper, finely chopped
    (about ⅓ cup)

2   medium green onions, sliced (about ¼ cup)

2   cans (4.5 ounces **each**) Swanson® Premium
    Chunk Chicken Breast, drained

    Sour cream for garnish

PREP
10 minutes

COOK
10 minutes

1. Heat the soup, milk, picante sauce, pepper and green
onions in a 2-quart saucepan over medium-high heat to
a boil, stirring often. Reduce the heat to low. Cook for
5 minutes, stirring often.

2. Add the chicken and heat through. Garnish with sour
cream.

Mexican Beef Stew

PREP
10 minutes

COOK
30 minutes

1½ pounds ground beef

1 large onion, chopped (about 1 cup)

½ teaspoon garlic powder **or** 2 cloves garlic, minced

1 can (10¾ ounces) Campbell's® Condensed Tomato Soup

1 can (10½ ounces) Campbell's® Condensed Beef Broth

1 cup water

2 tablespoons chili powder

3 medium potatoes, peeled and cut into cubes

1 can (about 16 ounces) whole kernel corn, drained

Shredded Cheddar cheese

1. Cook the beef, onion and garlic powder in a 12-inch skillet in 2 batches until it's well browned, stirring frequently to break up meat. Pour off any fat.

2. Stir the soup, broth, water, chili powder and potatoes into the skillet. Heat to a boil. Reduce the heat to low. Cover and cook for 15 minutes or until the potatoes are tender.

3. Stir the corn into the skillet. Cook and stir until hot and bubbling. Top with the cheese.

Hearty Lasagna Soup

1	pound ground beef
¼	teaspoon garlic powder
3½	cups Swanson® Seasoned Beef Broth with Onion
1	can (14½ ounces) diced tomatoes
¼	teaspoon dried Italian seasoning, crushed
1½	cups **uncooked** mafalda **or** corkscrew-shaped pasta (rotini)
¼	cup grated Parmesan cheese

PREP
5 minutes

COOK
25 minutes

1. Cook the beef with garlic powder in a 10-inch skillet over medium-high heat until it's well browned, stirring frequently to break up meat. Pour off any fat.

2. Stir the broth, tomatoes and Italian seasoning into the skillet. Heat to a boil.

3. Stir the pasta into the skillet. Reduce the heat to medium. Cook and stir for 10 minutes or until the pasta is tender. Stir in the cheese. Serve with additional cheese, if desired.

Easy Mushroom Soup

MAKES 4 SERVINGS

PREP
15 minutes

COOK
25 minutes

1¾ cups Swanson® Beef Broth (Regular, Lower Sodium **or** Certified Organic)

1¾ cups Swanson® Chicken Broth (Regular, Natural Goodness™ **or** Certified Organic)

⅛ teaspoon ground black pepper

⅛ teaspoon dried rosemary leaves, crushed

8 ounces fresh mushrooms, sliced (about 2 cups)

¼ cup thinly sliced carrots

¼ cup finely chopped onion

¼ cup sliced celery

¼ cup frozen peas

1 tablespoon sliced green onion

1. Heat the broth, black pepper, rosemary, mushrooms, carrots, onion, celery and peas in a 4-quart saucepan over medium heat to a boil. Reduce the heat to low. Cover and cook for 15 minutes.

2. Add the green onion. Cook for 5 minutes more or until the vegetables are tender.

Speedy Sides

Side dishes are a snap to prepare
when ingredients are on hand

Creamy Corn and Vegetable Orzo

PREP
10 minutes

COOK
10 minutes

2 tablespoons butter

4 medium green onions, sliced (about ½ cup)

2 cups frozen whole kernel corn

1 package (10 ounces) frozen vegetable (chopped broccoli, peas, sliced carrots **or** cut green beans)

½ of a 16-ounce package rice-shaped pasta (orzo), cooked and drained

1 can (10¾ ounces) Campbell's® Condensed Cream of Celery Soup (Regular **or** 98% Fat Free)

½ cup water

TIME-SAVING TIP

To quickly peel onions, pour boiling water over onions and let stand for 5 minutes. Then slip off skins.

1. Heat the butter in a 12-inch skillet over medium heat. Add the green onions and cook until tender. Add the corn, vegetable and pasta. Cook and stir for 3 minutes.

2. Stir the soup and water into the skillet. Cook and stir for 5 minutes or until mixture is hot and bubbling. Serve immediately.

Glazed Vegetables

PREP
20 minutes

COOK
15 minutes

2   tablespoons cornstarch

1¾ cups Swanson® Vegetable Broth (Regular **or** Certified Organic)

½   teaspoon ground ginger

¼   teaspoon garlic powder **or** 2 cloves garlic, minced

2   medium carrots, sliced (about 1 cup)

2   stalks celery, sliced (about 1 cup)

1   small red **or** green pepper, cut into 2-inch-long strips (about 1 cup)

1   large onion, cut into wedges

1   cup fresh **or** frozen broccoli flowerets

4   ounces snow peas

1. Stir the cornstarch and ¼ **cup** of the broth in a small bowl. Set the mixture aside.

2. Heat the remaining broth, ginger, garlic powder, carrots, celery, pepper, onion, broccoli and snow peas in a 12-inch skillet over medium-high heat to a boil. Reduce the heat to medium. Cover and cook for 5 minutes or until the vegetables are tender-crisp.

3. Stir the cornstarch mixture and stir it into the skillet. Cook and stir until the mixture boils and thickens.

Broccoli & Noodles Supreme

PREP
10 minutes

COOK
20 minutes

3 cups **uncooked** medium egg noodles

2 cups fresh **or** frozen broccoli flowerets

1 can (10¾ ounces) Campbell's® Condensed Cream of Chicken Soup (Regular **or** 98% Fat Free)

½ cup sour cream

⅓ cup grated Parmesan cheese

⅛ teaspoon ground black pepper

1. Prepare the noodles according to the package directions in a 4-quart saucepan. Add the broccoli during the last 5 minutes of the cooking time. Drain the noodles and broccoli well in a colander and return them to the saucepan.

2. Stir the soup, sour cream, cheese and black pepper into the noodles and broccoli. Cook and stir over medium heat until hot. Top with additional cheese before serving.

Cheesy Broccoli Potato Topper

PREP/COOK
10 minutes

4   hot baked potatoes, split

1   cup cooked broccoli flowerets

1   can (10¾ ounces) Campbell's® Condensed Cheddar Cheese Soup

1. Place the potatoes on a microwavable plate. Fluff up the potatoes with a fork. Divide the broccoli among the potatoes.

2. Stir the soup in the can with a spoon until it's smooth. Spoon the soup over the filled potatoes. Microwave on HIGH for 4 minutes or until they're hot.

New Potatoes and Peas

MAKES 7 SERVINGS

9   small new potatoes, cut into quarters
    (about 1½ pounds)

1   can (10¾ ounces) Campbell's® Condensed
    Cream of Mushroom Soup (Regular
    or 98% Fat Free)

⅓   cup milk

½   teaspoon dried thyme leaves **or** dill weed,
    crushed

⅛   teaspoon ground black pepper

1   package (10 ounces) frozen peas, thawed
    and drained

PREP
10 minutes

COOK
20 minutes

1. Place the potatoes in a 3-quart saucepan. Add water
to cover and heat over high heat to a boil. Reduce the
heat to low. Cover and cook for 8 minutes or until the
potatoes are fork-tender. Drain the potatoes in a
colander.

2. Stir the soup, milk, thyme, black pepper and peas
into the saucepan. Return the potatoes to the saucepan.
Cook and stir over low heat or until hot and bubbling.

Cheddar Potato Whip

PREP
5 minutes

COOK
25 minutes

2   pounds all-purpose potatoes, peeled
      and cut into 1-inch pieces (5 cups)

2   tablespoons butter

1   can (10¾ ounces) Campbell's® Condensed
      Cheddar Cheese Soup

⅓   cup sour cream

¼   teaspoon garlic powder
      Generous dash ground black pepper

1   medium green onion, chopped (about
      2 tablespoons)

EASY SUBSTITUTION TIP

*Use Campbell's®
Condensed Cream
of Mushroom Soup
for the Cheddar
Cheese Soup.*

1. Place the potatoes in a 3-quart saucepan. Add water to cover and heat over high heat to a boil. Reduce the heat to low. Cover and cook for 10 minutes or until the potatoes are tender. Drain the potatoes well in a colander.

2. Mash the potatoes with the butter. Stir in the soup, sour cream, garlic powder, black pepper and green onion.

Creamy 3-Cheese Pasta

MAKES 4 SERVINGS

PREP
20 minutes

BAKE
20 minutes

1   can (10¾ ounces) Campbell's® Condensed Cream of Mushroom Soup (Regular **or** 98% Fat Free)

1   cup milk

¼   teaspoon ground black pepper

1   package (8 ounces) shredded two-cheese blend

⅓   cup grated Parmesan cheese

3   cups corkscrew-shaped pasta (rotini), cooked and drained

1. Stir the soup, milk, black pepper and cheeses in a 1½-quart casserole. Stir in the pasta.

2. Bake at 400°F. for 20 minutes or until hot.

3. Stir before serving.

Easy Spinach Stuffing Casserole

PREP
10 minutes

BAKE
35 minutes

4 cups Pepperidge Farm® Herb Seasoned
    Stuffing

1 tablespoon butter, melted

1 can (10¾ ounces) Campbell's® Condensed
    Cream of Celery Soup (Regular **or**
    98% Fat Free)

½ cup sour cream

1 teaspoon onion powder

1 package (about 10 ounces) frozen spinach
    leaves, thawed, chopped and drained

¼ cup grated Parmesan cheese

1. Mix ½ **cup** of the stuffing and butter in a small bowl.

2. Stir the soup, sour cream, onion powder, spinach
and cheese in a medium bowl. Add the remaining
stuffing and stir lightly to coat.

3. Spoon into a 1½-quart casserole. Sprinkle with the
reserved stuffing mixture.

4. Bake at 350°F. for 35 minutes or until hot and topping
is golden.

Mushroom-Broccoli Alfredo

MAKES 4 SERVINGS

2 tablespoons butter

3 cups broccoli flowerets

3 cups sliced mushrooms

1 medium onion, coarsely chopped
   (about ½ cup)

½ teaspoon garlic powder **or** 2 cloves garlic,
   minced

1 can (10¾ ounces) Campbell's® Condensed
   Cream of Mushroom Soup (Regular
   or 98% Fat Free)

⅓ cup milk

2 tablespoons grated Parmesan cheese

⅛ teaspoon ground black pepper

½ of a 16-ounce package fettuccine **or** spaghetti
   pasta, cooked and drained

PREP
10 minutes

COOK
25 minutes

1. Heat the butter in a 10-inch skillet over medium heat.
Add the broccoli, mushrooms, onion and garlic powder.
Cook until the vegetables are tender-crisp.

2. Stir the soup, milk, cheese and black pepper into
the skillet. Cook and stir until the mixture is hot and
bubbling.

3. Place the pasta in a medium serving bowl. Pour
the soup mixture over pasta. Toss to coat.

Basil Skillet Potatoes

PREP
20 minutes

COOK
15 minutes

1   tablespoon butter

1   small onion, chopped (about ¼ cup)

½   teaspoon dried basil leaves, crushed

1   can (10¾ ounces) Campbell's® Condensed Cream of Celery Soup (Regular **or** 98% Fat Free)

¼   cup water

½   cup shredded Cheddar cheese

4   medium potatoes (about 1¼ pounds), cooked and sliced ¼ inch thick

1. Heat the butter in a 12-inch skillet over medium heat. Add the onion and basil and cook until tender.

2. Stir the soup, water and cheese into the skillet. Cook and stir until the cheese melts. Add the potatoes. Reduce the heat to low. Cook and gently stir to coat.

Vegetable-Rice Pilaf

1 tablespoon butter

¾ cup **uncooked** regular long-grain white rice

1¾ cups Swanson® Vegetable Broth (Regular **or** Certified Organic)

¼ teaspoon dried basil leaves, crushed

¾ cup frozen mixed vegetables

¼ cup chopped green **or** red pepper

PREP
5 minutes

COOK
25 minutes

1. Heat the butter in a 2-quart saucepan over medium-high heat. Add the rice and cook for 30 seconds or until the rice is browned, stirring constantly.

2. Stir in the broth and basil and heat to a boil. Reduce the heat to low. Cover the saucepan and cook for 10 minutes.

3. Stir in the vegetables and pepper. Cover and cook 10 minutes more or until the rice is tender and most of the liquid is absorbed.

Finishing Touches

Planning for dessert
has never been easier

Chocolate-Cinnamon Bread Pudding

PREP
15 minutes

BAKE
40 minutes

12 slices Pepperidge Farm® Cinnamon Swirl Bread, any variety, cut into cubes
½ cup semi-sweet chocolate pieces
2½ cups milk
4 eggs
½ cup packed brown sugar
1 teaspoon vanilla extract
Sweetened whipped cream (optional)

EASY SUBSTITUTION TIP

Use raisins for the chocolate pieces.

1. Place the bread cubes in a greased 12×8×2-inch shallow baking dish. Sprinkle the chocolate pieces over the bread cubes. Beat the milk, eggs, sugar and vanilla. Pour over the bread cubes.

2. Bake at 350°F. for 40 minutes or until a knife inserted near the center comes out clean. Serve warm with the whipped cream, if desired.

Glazed Peach Dumplings

THAW
40 minutes

PREP
10 minutes

BAKE
20 minutes

COOL
10 minutes

½ of a 17.3-ounce package Pepperidge Farm® Frozen Puff Pastry Sheets (1 sheet)

1 egg

1 tablespoon water

2 cans (about 29 ounces **each**) yellow cling peach halves

2 tablespoons packed brown sugar

2 tablespoons chopped pecans

Confectioners' sugar

Vanilla ice cream

1. Thaw the pastry sheet at room temperature for 40 minutes or until it's easy to handle. Heat the oven to 375°F. Stir the egg and water with a fork in a small bowl.

2. Remove **6** peach halves and drain well on paper towels. Reserve remaining peaches for another use.

3. Unfold the pastry sheet on a lightly floured surface. Roll the sheet into a 12-inch square. Cut pastry into 6 (4-inch) squares. Press each square into a one section of a 3-inch muffin pan.

4. Place peach halves, cut-side up, into the pastry cup. Sprinkle **each** peach with **1 teaspoon each** brown sugar and pecans. Bring pastry sides up to almost enclose the peach. Brush pastry with the egg mixture.

5. Bake for 20 minutes or until golden brown. Remove from the pan and cool slightly on a wire rack. Sprinkle with confectioners' sugar. Serve warm with ice cream.

Puddin' & Pastries

BAKE
30 minutes

PREP
15 minutes

REFRIGERATE
30 minutes

1   package (10 ounces) Pepperidge Farm®
    Frozen Puff Pastry Shells

1   package (about 3.4 ounces) chocolate,
    vanilla **or** lemon instant pudding mix

1½ cups cold milk

1   container (8 ounces) frozen whipped topping,
    thawed

1. Bake and cool the pastry shells according to the package directions.

2. Prepare the pudding mix using the milk according to the package directions using **1½ cups** milk. Fold in **1 cup** of the whipped topping. Refrigerate 30 minutes.

3. Spoon **about ½ cup** pudding mixture into each pastry shell. Serve with additional whipped topping.

Mango Milk Shakes

2 cups V8® V.Fusion™ Peach Mango **or**
V8 Splash® Tropical Blend Juice

1 cup vanilla ice cream

PREP
5 minutes

Put the juice and ice cream in an electric blender
container. Cover and blend until smooth. Serve
immediately.

Sugar & Spice Pastry Straws

THAW
40 minutes

PREP
30 minutes

REFRIGERATE
1 hour
30 minutes

BAKE
20 minutes

½ of a 17.3-ounce package Pepperidge Farm® Frozen Puff Pastry Sheets (1 sheet)

1 egg, beaten

Generous dash salt

⅔ cup pecan halves, finely chopped

½ cup sugar

½ teaspoon ground cinnamon

1. Thaw the pastry sheet at room temperature for 40 minutes or until it's easy to handle. Line a 15×10-inch jelly roll pan with parchment paper or aluminum foil. Stir the egg and salt with a fork in a small bowl.

2. Unfold the pastry on a lightly floured surface. Roll the sheet into a 12-inch square. Brush pastry with the egg mixture.

3. Mix the pecans, sugar and cinnamon in a small bowl. Sprinkle the nut mixture over **half** of the pastry. Fold the other pastry half over the nut filling. Slide onto a pan and refrigerate 30 minutes or until the pastry is firm.

4. Roll the pastry on a lightly floured surface into a 12-inch square. Use a pizza cutter to cut the dough crosswise into 24 (about ½-inch-wide) strips. Twist the top of each strip in one direction and the bottom in an opposite direction several times to form a corkscrew shape. Place each twist, 2 inches apart, across the width (10-inch side) of the prepared pan. Press the ends of each twist against the sides of the pan so they stick. (This keeps the twists from unraveling while they are baking.) Refrigerate for 1 hour.

5. Heat the oven to 350°F. Bake for 20 minutes or until golden and well caramelized. Cool in pan on a wire rack for 5 minutes. While the twists are still flexible and before they cool completely, trim the ends with a sharp knife. If you wish, cut the twists in half. Serve with a creamy dessert or as a tea pastry. Store twists between sheets of waxed paper in an airtight container.

Fruit Pizza Puff

MAKES 16 SERVINGS

1   package (17.3 ounces) Pepperidge Farm®
    Frozen Puff Pastry Sheets (2 sheets)
1   package (3.4 ounces) vanilla instant
    pudding mix
2   cups cold milk
4   cups assorted fresh fruit (sliced strawberries,
    kiwis, raspberries **and/or** blueberries)

THAW
    40 minutes

PREP
    30 minutes

BAKE
    20 minutes

COOL
    30 minutes

1. Thaw the pastry sheets at room temperature for
40 minutes or until they're easy to handle. Heat the
oven to 400°F.

2. Unfold the pastry sheets on a lightly floured surface.
Roll each sheet into a 12-inch square. Cut off the
corners to make a circle. Gently press the dough with
lightly floured fingers into a 12-inch circle. Place each
pastry round on an ungreased baking sheet or pizza
pan. Prick the pastry rounds all over with a fork.

3. Bake for 20 minutes or until golden. Remove the
pastries from the baking sheets and cool them on wire
racks.

4. Prepare the pudding mix using the milk according
to the package directions. Spoon **1 cup** of the pudding
onto each crust and spread to within ½ inch of the
edges. Arrange the fruit over the pudding. Cut each
pizza into 8 wedges and serve immediately, or cover
and refrigerate the pizzas for up to 4 hours.

Cooking for a Crowd: Recipe may be doubled.
Double all ingredients.

Chocolate Mousse Napoleons with Strawberries & Cream

MAKES 8 NAPOLEONS

THAW
40 minutes

PREP
25 minutes

BAKE
12 minutes

½ of a 17.3-ounce package Pepperidge Farm® Frozen Puff Pastry Sheets (1 sheet)
1 cup heavy cream
  Confectioners' sugar
½ teaspoon vanilla extract
⅔ cup semi-sweet chocolate pieces, melted and cooled
1¼ cups strawberries

EASY SUBSTITUTION TIP

Substitute 2 cups thawed frozen whipped topping for the heavy cream. Omit the confectioners' sugar and vanilla.

---

1. Thaw the pastry sheet at room temperature for 40 minutes or until it's easy to handle. Heat the oven to 400°F.

2. Unfold the pastry on a lightly floured surface. Cut into 3 strips along fold marks. Cut each strip into 4 rectangles. Place 1 inch apart on baking sheet.

3. Bake for 12 minutes or until golden. Remove from baking sheet and cool on wire rack.

4. Beat the cream, **1 tablespoon** confectioners' sugar and vanilla with electric mixer at high speed until soft peaks form. Divide the cream mixture in half. Fold ⅓ **cup** of the melted chocolate into one half. Reserve the remaining chocolate for the garnish. Split the pastries into 2 layers, making 24.

5. Spread 8 pastry layers with the chocolate cream mixture and top with 8 pastry layers. Top with remaining whipped cream, strawberries and remaining pastry layers. Sprinkle with additional confectioners' sugar. Drizzle with remaining chocolate. Serve immediately or refrigerate up to 4 hours.

Chocolate Triangles

MAKES 32 PASTRIES

1 package (17.3 ounces) Pepperidge Farm®
  Frozen Puff Pastry Sheets (2 sheets)
2 egg yolks, beaten
2 teaspoons water
¾ cup semi-sweet chocolate pieces **or** chunks
  Confectioners' sugar

THAW
40 minutes

PREP
25 minutes

FREEZE
15 minutes

BAKE
15 minutes

COOL
10 minutes

1. Thaw the pastry sheets at room temperature for 40 minutes or until they're easy to handle. Heat the oven to 375°F. Stir the egg yolks and water with a fork in a cup.

2. Unfold **1** pastry sheet on a lightly floured surface. Roll the sheet into a 16-inch square. Brush the pastry lightly with some of the egg mixture. Cut the pastry sheet into 16 (4-inch) squares.

3. Put **1 teaspoon** chocolate pieces onto the center of each square. Fold the pastry over the filling to form a triangle and press the edges together to seal. Press the sealed edges with the tines of a fork. Prick the center of each triangle. Repeat with remaining pastry and chocolate pieces. Put triangles on a shallow-sided baking pan. Brush triangles with egg mixture. Freeze triangles for 15 minutes or until firm. Put triangles on 2 ungreased baking sheets.

4. Bake for 15 minutes or until the triangles are puffed and golden. Remove the triangles from the baking sheet and cool slightly on wire rack. Sprinkle triangles with confectioners' sugar. Serve warm.

Chocolate-Raspberry Triangles: Put 1 fresh raspberry with the chocolate pieces on the center of each pastry square before folding.

Pear Tortetta

PREP
40 minutes

COOK/BAKE
33 minutes

COOL
5 minutes

½ of a 17.3-ounce package Pepperidge Farm® Frozen Puff Pastry Sheets (1 sheet)

⅓ cup granulated sugar

⅓ cup packed brown sugar

½ teaspoon ground cinnamon

4 to 5 medium ripe pears, peeled, cored and cut in half

2 tablespoons fresh lemon juice

3 tablespoons butter, softened

1. Thaw the pastry sheet at room temperature for 40 minutes or until it's easy to handle. Heat the oven to 425°F.

2. Mix the granulated sugar, brown sugar and cinnamon in a small bowl. Set aside.

3. Brush the pears with the lemon juice.

4. Spread the butter in the bottom of a 10-inch oven-safe skillet. Sprinkle the sugar mixture into the pan. Arrange the pear halves, cut-side up, with the tapered end of the pear towards the center of the pan. Cook over medium heat for about 8 minutes or until the mixture thickens and the sugar melts. Remove from the heat.

5. Unfold the pastry sheet on a lightly floured surface. Roll the sheet into a 13-inch circle. Place the pastry over the pears to cover and tuck in the sides around the pears slightly.

6. Bake for 25 minutes or until puffed and golden. Place on a wire rack to cool for 5 minutes. Place a serving platter over the skillet and carefully flip the skillet upside down to invert the tart onto the plate. Serve warm.

Palmiers

1 package (17.3 ounces) Pepperidge Farm®
  Frozen Puff Pastry Sheets (2 sheets)
1 egg
1 tablespoon water
6 tablespoons sugar
1 cup semi-sweet chocolate pieces, melted

THAW
40 minutes

PREP
20 minutes

BAKE
12 minutes

1. Thaw the pastry sheets at room temperature for 40 minutes until they're easy to handle. Heat the oven to 400°F. Lightly grease 2 baking sheets. Stir the egg and water with a fork in small bowl.

2. Unfold **1** pastry sheet on a lightly floured surface. Roll the sheet into a 16×10-inch rectangle. Brush with egg mixture. Sprinkle with **2 tablespoons** sugar. Starting at the short sides, fold pastry toward center, leaving a ¼-inch space in the center. Brush with egg mixture and sprinkle with **1 tablespoon** sugar. Fold one side over the other, making a 4-layer rectangle. Repeat with remaining pastry sheet.

3. Cut each rectangle into 12 (¾-inch) slices. Place cut-side down 2 inches apart on prepared baking sheets. Brush tops with egg mixture.

4. Bake for 12 minutes or until golden. Remove from the baking sheets and cool on a wire rack.

5. Dip half of each palmier into chocolate. Place on waxed paper-lined baking sheets. Refrigerate until the chocolate is set.

Easy Fruit Shells

PREP
20 minutes

BAKE
30 minutes

1   package (10 ounces) Pepperidge Farm®
    Frozen Puff Pastry Shells

1   package (3.4 ounces) vanilla instant pudding
    mix

2   cups cold milk

2   cups cut-up fresh fruit (bananas, strawberries
    and/or grapes)
    Whipped topping

1. Bake and cool the pastry shells according to the package directions.

2. Prepare the pudding mix using the milk according to the package directions.

3. Spoon **about ⅓ cup** of the pudding into each pastry shell. Top with the fruit. Serve with whipped topping. Serve immediately or cover and refrigerate up to 4 hours before serving.

index